# Understanding
## and
# Clarifying Your Values
## (Assessment Included)

---

## William O. Blackwood
## L. Ray Mauser

---

ISBN:        1475108621

ISBN 13:   9781475108620

*For the many executives and managers who have shared their beliefs and taught us much about values and value-based leadership during coaching and workshops.*

# Table of Contents

# Preface

As executive coaches, we have long sought a better foundational source for helping people gain greater insight into their values. Rather than continuing to search for a practical, insightful way to help each individual clarify, understand, and apply his or her values, we decided, based on our years of experience in the field, to create this book, which includes an assessment, as a helpful guide.

Values tell us what is important. We all have a personal set of values that guides our behavior. How consistently we behave with a personal value reflects how important that value is to us. Complicating the matter are the various social roles in which we find ourselves (mother, manager, husband, teacher, and so forth), each of which has values attached to it that guide our behavior to some degree. In cases where we do not agree with a value at all, we ignore it.

Several facets of values are not addressed in this book. Our values, for example, are sometimes coercive. That is, they compel us to favor certain social, political, or religious issues. But this topic is beyond the scope of this book. Values, moreover, are linked to ethical and moral precepts. But, again, this topic is not addressed here. Knowing our values strongly influences how we establish personal and organizational goals and visualizes the future, how we set strategies, and so forth. Although values-based leadership is another powerful leadership development topic, it is also outside the bounds of this book.

Finally, the assessment and exercises in this book were created with the reader in mind. By defining and providing synonyms for each value term, we aim to clarify each value choice presented.

# Introduction

## A. Why this Book

The intent of this book is to provide you with a process for clarifying your values. It also helps validate your values, and understand the ways you engage in value-driven actions in carrying out your roles and responsibilities. Personal values guide our behavior and color how we interpret values attached to other roles.

As executive coaches, our focus has been on executives and leaders; however, the assessment and exercises in this book have broad applicability to any reader desiring to know or clarify his or her personal values.

Although each of us has a set of values that defines and guides our behavior and actions in the short term, how we prioritize values is different for each person. Values change over time, as do their relative importance to us. The more important a value is to us, the more likely we are to behave consistently with the value. As a result, values need to be periodically checked to determine their relative importance to us. Thus, the material in this book will help you to identify, clarify, and prioritize your values.

Readers will better understand their underlying value orientation and know what values are most important to them. Values drive how one gathers and interprets data, frames decisions, and makes choices. Moreover, understanding values is essential to understanding human behavior. Rokeach (1973) asserts that values are enduring beliefs about a specific mode of conduct that is personally or socially preferable to an opposite or converse mode or conduct of existence. Values also impact how you select action, evaluate people and events, and explain your actions and evaluations (Kluckhohn 1951; Rokeach 1973; Schwartz 1992). Consequently, our personal values strongly color our behavior and actions and do matter to each of us, especially those in leader or manager roles.

## B. "In a Nutshell"

First, we discuss values, in general, by clarifying what values are, and then we further define values. We distinguish values from other concepts, such as behaviors, attitudes, and attributes, by providing you with a value clarification exercise followed by ways to actually validate your selection. Throughout this book, we stress the importance of values and how they impact your daily judgment, choices, and decisions, both at work and at home.

We also show how values drive you in your daily activities—that is, how your values color your perceptions, aid in decision making, help set a direction or create a vision, establish priorities, and create personal value-driven goals.

## C. Why Values Matter

"MAN, HOWEVER, IS ABLE TO LIVE AND EVEN TO DIE FOR THE SAKE OF HIS IDEALS AND VALUES!"

— (VIKTOR E. FRANKL, 2006)

Our conduct and choices are based on values, which constitute our beliefs about what is important to us. The relevance of values cannot be argued, as we humans have struggled with determining right from wrong and good from evil since the beginning of time.

Values, which influence your choices about where to invest your time and energy, are what you believe are important.

Values provide a strong foundation, a method for living your life to its fullest. If you are already familiar with your values, then it is a good idea to periodically confirm these values have not shifted or changed.

Values also filter our judgments, and they either help or hinder us and influence the way we feel and think about something or someone. The way we behave and how we react emotionally to the world around us is driven in part by our deeply held values. Values reflect one's judgment and help sort out what is important. It is difficult to accomplish goals if there is a conflict with an internal value.

Moreover, values help us to get and stay motivated and energized. For example, we are motivated to take our lives in certain directions through our choices, which are determined in part by the values we hold most meaningful at that time. Thus, values are used as our guiding principles. What is important to you? What is important about your work and home life? Do your work and non-work values align? Clarifying your values will help in answering these questions.

According to Abraham Maslow (1954), values perform three primary functions: they help us defend against perceived threats, adjust to society, and foster growth. When we consider these three functions, we understand why values are essential; values truly matter to us. These functions are relevant not only for individuals, but also for interpersonal relationships, teams, and organizations.

# 1

# When Do Values Matter?

Our values, which impact our thoughts and behaviors, matter when we engage in the following:

## A. Evaluating Our Choices

We judge and evaluate a person or situation based on available choices requiring us to reach a final conclusion or choice. Our thought process and choices are value-driven, as is the final choice selected, and our internally held values are major undercurrents affecting our judgment and, ultimately, our choices. In this light, judgment impacts our reasoning.

In short, our values serve as guides when we make decisions, and they color our perceptions and consequent behaviors.

## B. Influencing and Persuading

Other people sense not only our credibility but also our conviction. Thus, knowing our values strengthens our ability to influence and persuade others.

## C. Generating Clarity around Goals and Objectives

It is difficult to achieve our goals or objectives if our internal values are in conflict with those goals. Internally we are affirming one thing, yet externally we are acting in opposition. Knowing our values will help us clarify where we are headed and ensure values and goals are congruent.

## |D. Reducing Conflict and Stress

If we clearly know and can verbalize our values, we can avoid conflict over choices and dilemmas. Dissonance and stress often result from conflicts in making choices about values that seem equally important. College roommates, for example, often disagree on the slob-neat-freak continuum. Punctuality can be another point of disagreement. Our ability to frame differences leading to conflict can make us more influential and effective in reducing conflict.

## |E. Internal Guide to Actions

When we are unclear about what values we hold dear, we can be tempted to engage in actions and activities that clearly are not in our best interest. People of good character know their values and will not easily violate these values because values serve as internal guides that direct their behavior.

# II

# Other Classifications of Values

Because our focus is on personal values, one might ask why we included this section on social roles and aspirational values. We added it because it reinforces your social roles. In addition, it identifies the notion of aspirational values that we possess as individuals. It also flags a term we hear often: core values.

Rokeach (1973) defines core values as enduring beliefs that a specific mode of conduct or end-state of existence is personally or socially preferable to an opposite or converse mode of conduct or end-state of existence. Lencioni (2002b) discusses core values within an organizational context (see references).

## A. Values and Social Roles

Our personal values often overlap with other types of values. These categories depend on a large extent on our social role. In order to understand how a particular value is affecting our decisions and behaviors, it is necessary to understand the context (i.e., the social or aspirational role) in which we are operating. If, for example, the value is personal, it may be viewed and employed differently in our family role versus our office management role. Also, societal expectations may influence values associated with our ambitions and our social, economic, and professional roles. While the following categories are not exhaustive, they do capture the majority of value types:

1. **Personal** values are ours as individuals and typically reflect our moral character. They often include honesty, loyalty, responsibility, self-satisfaction, and so forth.

2. **Social** values are learned and represent values people expect out of habit, morals, legal issues, and taboos (dos and don'ts of a particular society). They typically include equality, justice, liberty, and freedom.

3. **Aspirational** values are what we hold for the future. When asked to identify their values, many individuals respond with what they would like those values to be. Aspirational values can become core values over time, but they

can also dilute core values and cause confusion over what is organizationally important. As noted above, these are often a future-looking mix of personal and social values depicting what one would like to become, or values that involve self-improvement. In this latter context, one's values might be associated with achievement, influence, wealth, and so forth.

4. **Political** values are associated with a political party, but they also may include public service, voting, democracy, civic responsibility, and so forth.

5. **Economic** values may include pride of ownership, money, private property, distribution of wealth, and equal employment.

6. **Religious** values are formed during spiritual education wherever it takes place (home, church, synagogue, etc.) and include freedom to worship, human dignity, reverence for life, belief in a Supreme Being, and faith.

7. **Managerial or organizational** values are usually generated and publicized by organizational leaders. They often include values such as fact-based decision-making, fast response, future focus, continuous learning, customer service, and teamwork.

8. **Professional** values are associated with medical, legal, finance, engineering, and coaching professions (see appendix 1).

# III

# Defining and Distinguishing Values

## A. Values Defined

Values are defined as principles that one holds as appropriate and important. Values are principles that people will defend. Further, people's values typically predict their short-term behavior, and they often change over time. In short, values are principles—those psychological paradigms or constructs—that you believe are important or worthwhile and are willing to defend. They influence the way you act, the way you dress, who your friends are, your self-confidence, and your beliefs. Values are, in essence, your very being.

Values are what you believe are meaningfully important and influence your choices about where to invest your time and energy. People will defend their values and use them to achieve short-term objectives. Values are as much emotional as they are intellectual and so will resonate with you or make you receptive or responsive to something.

## B. Virtues

Virtues are often confused with values. To clarify, virtues are used to describe someone of an upright and high moral character (i.e., a virtuous person). Often seen as a sole value (virtuous), it is better defined by a set of values such as integrity, honesty, fairness, competence, respect, accountability, trustworthiness, caring, and so forth. The *Oxford Dictionary of Philosophy* edited by Blackburn (2005) defines a virtue as a *trait* of character that is to be admired, one rendering its possessor better—either morally or intellectually—in his or her conduct of specific affairs.

## C. Distinguishing Behaviors, Attributes, Traits, and Attitudes

Values are often confused with other terms besides virtues. Below, we distinguish values from these other terms. That said, we do not make a distinction between values and beliefs because they are largely synonymous.

9

We include and explain terms that may not, by definition, be values listed in appendix 2. For example, other value lists frequently include terms identifying behaviors, attributes, attitudes, traits, and so forth, which are often confusing to those trying to clarify their values. While some of these terms remain open to debate, we have attempted to distinguish them. If you believe a term included in the behaviors or attributes category in appendix 2 is still a meaningful value to you, then by all means include it in your value list.

Nevertheless, many terms are cited as values that should belong in another category. Below are several categories that include terms commonly cited as values:

## 1. Behaviors

Behaviors are your observable or recordable actions or reactions in response to external or internal stimuli. Although other people can observe your behaviors, no one can observe your values, which are internal and therefore hidden. According to *Webster's New World Dictionary*, behavior is the way people act, how they conduct themselves, or how they function.

## 2. Traits

Richard E. Boyatzis (1982, 28) cites David McClelland (1951) as describing a trait as "a dispositional or characteristic way in which the person responds to an equivalent set of stimuli." An example of a trait is good hand–eye coordination. Similarly, *Webster's New World Dictionary* defines a trait as a distinguishing quality or characteristic such as personality.

## 3. Attributes

An attribute is an inherent personal quality or characteristic. The distinction is that attributes are often used to describe someone else, whether the person being described agrees with it or not. Take, for example, the co-worker who is an unusually quick thinker or the colleague who is very candid. An attribute, according to *Webster's Encyclopedic Unabridged Dictionary*, is something attributed by way of belonging or to consider as belonging to something. For, example, he attributed intelligence to his colleague.

## 4. Attitudes

Dr. Niaomi Rotter, Professor of Management, New Jersey Institute of Technology, says attitudes are a "stable cluster of feelings and behavioral intentions towards specific people, things, or events." See NJIT website in references.

*Webster's Encyclopedic Unabridged Dictionary* defines an attitude as a tendency or orientation toward a person or thing, whereas the *Oxford Dictionary of Philosophy* (2nd ed.) describes an attitude as an evaluative response, usually contrasted with simple belief by its more direct connection with motivation and behavior. It is a state of contentment or active discontent with the way some things are.

An attitude, for instance, is a disposition or tendency representing an individual's *degree* of like, dislike, or ambivalence for an item, often representing a judgment. Your moods may reinforce certain attitudes. Moods unlike attitudes are far more transitory (hours or days).

The terms we've discussed thus far are summarized below.

# Summary to Distinguish between Terms

| Term | Definition |
|---|---|
| Values | Principles you believe are meaningfully important and influence your choices about where to invest your time and energy. Values, which predict our short-term behavior, are the principles we defend. |
| Virtues | Virtues are similar to attributes, which are used to *describe* someone; however, virtues are used specifically for describing moral character. Virtues describe someone of an upright and high moral character (i.e., a virtuous person). |
| Behaviors | Behaviors are your observable or recordable actions or reactions seen by others in response to external or internal stimuli. Other people can observe your behavior. A value, on the other hand, is internal and hidden. |
| Beliefs | Beliefs and values are synonymous. |
| Traits | Traits are a person's innate, observable characteristics. For example, a trait might be a person's good hand–eye coordination. Consider the following question: Is this a distinguishing characteristic or quality about someone, which is often seen as a peculiarity, such as unusual stamina? |
| Attributes | Attributes are used to describe someone else, whether the person being described agrees with this assessment or not. For example, he is an unusually quick thinker, or she is very honest. Not everyone necessarily agrees with a description you attribute to someone. |
| Attitudes | An attitude is a disposition or tendency representing an individual's degree of like, dislike, or ambivalence for an item; it often represents a judgment. Attitudes may be changed more easily through persuasion—as opposed to deeply held values, which an individual will defend. |
| Terms often viewed as values | In appendix 2, we've listed terms often viewed as values that do not fall into the above categories. Although these terms are frequently cited as values, they are simply typical ways, tests, or means for acquiring or accomplishing something. |

Appendix 2 lists these categories (other than values and beliefs) along with associated words and explanations. You may or may not agree with our categorization of terms in this appendix. If you disagree, we suggest you move the term back into your list of values for prioritization.

# IV

# Do Values Endure or Do They Change?

Our values do change over time and reflect what we hold to be important at that time. For instance, values for older people (e.g., faith, family, and health) may be different from the values they had when they were younger (e.g., achievement, autonomy, and adventure). Significant emotional events and incidents can cause changes in our values. Therefore, our values frequently change over our lifetime. Our core values remain mostly the same, but the values we prioritize may shift accordingly in and out of our top ten. This shift in value position means that we are not living as consistently with a particular value. A highly ranked value may mean that we are living consistently with it 80 percent of the time. For example, everyone lies. Perhaps it's just a little white lie to protect a loved one's feelings, but it is a lie nevertheless. Therefore, if someone ranks honesty as one of their top three values and then lies many times a day, one would have to question the ranking given the inconsistency in behavior.

It is important to note that when we are going through a transition period, we find it difficult to rank our values. The reason is that we are tottering between what we valued before and what our behaviors indicate we value now. But our new values and subsequent behaviors typically do not come as a bolt out of the blue. These were values that we considered important but were not yet living consistently with.

We have found during beta testing of the assessment instrument and follow-on discussions with clients that most people when questioned admit to not living with his or her values 100 percent of the time. Even if we are living consistently with our values 80 percent of the time, we are extraordinary. However, we often have values that rank in the lower third of our top ten that we are even living a lot less consistently with—often as low as 20% of the time.

Therefore, it is essential that each of us periodically clarifies and prioritizes our values. At some point, everyone will face value conflicts, but keep in mind that the choices we make live with us forever.

# V

# Values Clarification Exercise

Now it is time to clarify your personal values. You should be clear about what you value. Your values help you establish and achieve personal goals and dreams. For leaders numerous leadership styles are described in the literature, it is our values applied to those leadership styles that make us authentic leaders.

In *Values and Teaching*, Raths, Harmon, and Simon (1973) identify several criteria that together constitute a fully developed value. A value, they argue, must be chosen freely from alternatives after thoughtful consideration of the consequences of each alternative, and you must be happy with the choice and willing to affirm the choice publicly—that is, do something with the choice repeatedly, in some pattern of life. These yardsticks are worth considering as you go about clarifying your own personal values.

The following exercise involves four steps. First, narrow the list of values to your top twenty. Second, identify and rank your top ten from 1 (most important) to 10 (least important). Third, validate your top five with examples. Fourth, determine the five values your reject or are absolutely unimportant to you from the list provided. Finally, complete the Robin Hood exercise and rank the characters.

## A. Eliciting Your Values: Values Clarification Worksheet

We ask you to engage in a value clarification and prioritization exercise. Please set aside twenty to thirty minutes to complete this exercise, and do not rush; rather, be thoughtful and as honest with yourself as possible.

## B. Beginning Guidance

The following matrix lists seventy values. This list is not exhaustive; instead, it represents our experience in helping people clarify their strongest internally held values. Because these value terms may be interpreted differently, we provide an explanation for each.

We have tried to avoid duplication. Where we have chosen a value that closely relates to another term, we have tried to show it in the explanation column as a synonymous word. For example, achievement includes accomplishment, adaptable includes flexible, achievement includes ambition and aspiration, autonomy includes independence, compassion includes caring, fairness includes equality, and so forth. We encourage you to look carefully at the explanations to make sure a value you might be considering is not already in the explanation column.

You will also find numerous terms in appendix 2 that are often cited in lists of values in other references. If you are looking for a value you believe is meaningful but cannot find it in the matrix below, please look at the tables in appendix 2. If you find a personal value listed under behaviors, attributes, traits, and so forth, include it in your values prioritization list.

Using the values table below, identify your top twenty using the next to the last column by placing a check mark in the row indicating your chosen value. Next, in the last column, reduce your twenty down to ten, again using check marks. Please double-check that you are comfortable with your final top ten that they resonate and are truly meaningful to you.

Also, ensure the values you select are yours and not someone else's. That is, be sure your values are not what you think someone else wants you to have as values, or that you believe are important to others; they should be your values, and yours alone.

# Values Identification Matrix

| # | Value | Explanation | Top 20 | Top 10 |
|---|-------|-------------|--------|--------|
| 1 | Accountable | Willingness to accept responsibility; being liable for an action | | |
| 2 | Adaptable | Desire to be flexible or to modify behavior to fit changing circumstances | | |
| 3 | Achievement | Need for accomplishment; aspiring, ambitious, motivated, determined, and driven | | |
| 4 | Adventure | Need to undertake new, risky, and daring enterprises | | |
| 5 | Aesthetics | Desire for beautiful, artistic, pleasing things such as nature's splendor | | |
| 6 | Affiliation | Need to belong; fellowship and close personal ties | | |
| 7 | Altruism | Unselfish concern for others' interests, needs, and welfare | | |
| 8 | Autonomy | Need for independence; self-sufficiency and self-determination | | |
| 9 | Candor | Desire to be sincere, forthright, and open | | |
| 10 | Compassion | Wanting to care, show kindness to others, and wishing to relieve suffering | | |
| 11 | Confidence | Feeling self-assured, certain, poised in ability or action | | |
| 12 | Confidentiality | Desire for privacy and concealment, secrecy, discretion, and silence | | |
| 13 | Courage | Willing to face danger or fear with resolution, bravery | | |
| 14 | Determination | Need to be firm in will; strength, purpose of character, and dedicated | | |
| 15 | Diversity | Belief and respect for things that differ; variety | | |
| 16 | Empathy | Need to anticipate, identify, and meet the needs of others; understand, know, feel, and act on emotions in others | | |

| # | Value | Explanation | Top 20 | Top 10 |
|---|---|---|---|---|
| 17 | Excellence | Desire for high standard of quality, goodness, and superiority | | |
| 18 | Expertise | Need to gain high degree of knowledge, proficiency, or capability in topic | | |
| 19 | Fact-based decision making | Desire to be analytical, rational, and to make evidence-based choices | | |
| 20 | Faith | Confident belief in an idea, person, nation, spirit, or thing that cannot be confirmed | | |
| 21 | Fame | Need for distinctive reputation, renown, or prominence | | |
| 22 | Family | Need to be with loved ones; time with nearest kin | | |
| 23 | Fairness | Desire for equality, evenhandedness, impartiality, and justice | | |
| 24 | Forgiving | Inclination to stop blaming or being angry with someone | | |
| 25 | Fortitude | Belief in firmness of mind; suffer pain with stoic resolve, strength, and grit | | |
| 26 | Freedom | Need for free will; self-determination, lack of restrictions, and independence | | |
| 27 | Friendship | Belief in camaraderie, companionship, mutual esteem, and goodwill | | |
| 28 | Happiness | A life that goes well from the individual's perspective; desire for contentment and progress, cheerfulness, joy, and delight | | |
| 29 | Harmonious | Need for agreeableness, cordiality, and cooperation | | |
| 30 | Health | Desire for well-being, vigor, and fitness | | |
| 31 | Honesty | Wanting truthfulness, directness, accuracy, and sincerity in communication | | |
| 32 | Human dignity | Having respect for worth, goodness, and betterment of self and others | | |

| # | Value | Explanation | Top 20 | Top 10 |
|---|-------|-------------|--------|--------|
| 33 | Humility | Need for or preferring modesty; being unassuming and humble | | |
| 34 | Humor | Need for wittiness, fun, jocularity, or absurdity; seeing incongruity | | |
| 35 | Influence | Need for persuasiveness, clout, prerogative; winning over or inspiring | | |
| 36 | Initiative | Desire for starting activities some time in advance, which may or may not be obvious to others | | |
| 37 | Innovative | Need to have pioneering, original, or novel ideas or approaches to problems | | |
| 38 | Integrity | Consistency in personal actions and beliefs; upright constancy in personal actions; devoted to values and ideals whether or not accepted by others | | |
| 39 | Justice | Wants choices to conform to legal rightness in action or attitude; balanced | | |
| 40 | Liberty | Right to act, believe, or express yourself in a way of your own choosing | | |
| 41 | Loyalty | Need to be faithful and steadfast to your friends, organization, community or nation; devoted, displaying allegiance | | |
| 42 | Merciful | Need to show forgiveness to those you have the power to punish | | |
| 43 | Moral Courage | Need and willingness to publicly defend your values or moral principles over time in the face of danger | | |
| 44 | Optimism | Desire to envision the best possible outcome; hopeful, confident, or upbeat | | |
| 45 | Orderliness | Desire to be neat, tidy, uniform, and efficient | | |
| 46 | Patriotic | Need to demonstrate strong belief in national values; devotion and affection | | |

| # | Value | Explanation | Top 20 | Top 10 |
|---|-------|-------------|--------|--------|
| 47 | Peace | Need for a feeling of security, calmness, quietude, and freedom from strife, war, or violence | | |
| 48 | Perseverance | Need to persist in the face of adversity; resolve and resilience | | |
| 49 | Power | Desire and capacity to control or act effectively with dominance | | |
| 50 | Punctuality | Need to be on time for commitments or events; prompt with no delay | | |
| 51 | Recognition | Need for affirmation and acknowledgment | | |
| 52 | Reliability | Want dependability, consistency, predictability in others | | |
| 53 | Righteousness | Desire morally upright behavior without guilt or sin | | |
| 54 | Sacrifice | Willing to give up something for something else considered more important | | |
| 55 | Self-discipline | Need to be in control of yourself despite deliberate provocation | | |
| 56 | Simplicity | Need condition or quality judged to be uncomplicated or simple and easy to understand | | |
| 57 | Sincerity | Need for genuineness, earnestness, and freedom from duplicity | | |
| 58 | Service to others | Meeting the needs and supportive of clients, friends, and family | | |
| 59 | Privacy | Wanting time alone, space to yourself, solitude, or seclusion | | |
| 60 | Spirituality | Concerned with the soul and opposed to sensuality or worldliness | | |
| 61 | Stewardship | Need for careful conduct, supervision, or frugal management of resources | | |
| 62 | Teamwork | Desire for collaboration, joint effort, cooperative interaction with a group | | |
| 63 | Thrifty | Desire to be frugal, economical, and prudent | | |

| # | Value | Explanation | Top 20 | Top 10 |
|---|---|---|---|---|
| 64 | Tolerance | Broadmindedness and forbearance; respectful of others' beliefs or practices | | |
| 65 | Trustworthy | Wanting to be deserving of others' trust; predictable and warrants confidence | | |
| 66 | Truth | Desire for everyone to be accurate, factual, exact, forthright, and to show veracity | | |
| 67 | Understanding | Accepting, comprehending, but not necessarily acting | | |
| 68 | Variety | Desire for changing responsibilities, content, setting, or diversity | | |
| 69 | Wealth | Need for affluence; being financially independent, prosperous | | |
| 70 | Wisdom | Desire to be perceptive, insightful, have acumen, be astute | | |
| 71 | Other: | | | |
| 72 | Other: | | | |
| 73 | Other: | | | |

# VI

## Prioritizing Values

*"Courage is the first of human qualities because it is the quality which guarantees the others." (Winston Churchill, 1937)*

As you prioritize your values, do not be influenced by others or what you believe others want of you. For instance, the Churchill quote above seems logical until you ask, "Where does courage come from?"

We now ask you to prioritize your previously selected top ten values in order of importance to you.

If you find it difficult to prioritize all ten values, then, as a minimum, sort your highest five values in priority order and then list the last five of the ten as non-prioritized top values.

Also, if you have other high-priority values not listed in the table, please decide if they should be included as one or more of your top ten values; however, try not to interpret or co-mingle a behavior (see section III) as a value. Your values shape or drive your behaviors or the actions you take—not the other way around.

In priority order, the top things I personally value most in my life are

1. _____          6. _____

2. _____          7. _____

3. _____          8. _____

4. _____          9. _____

5. _____          10. _____

As you think about your top ten values, you should also consider whether each of your chosen values is meaningful and used often in your life. You should consider <u>why</u> these values are important to you (as opposed to just whether they are important) and how often those values are applied in your daily personal and professional decisions.

Next, please consider the rejected values. Please return to the list of values shown in the matrix and identify the five values that are of no importance to you. You do not have to prioritize these values, but you do need to know what these values are because they may affect your interaction with others.

1. _____

2. _____

3. _____

4. _____

5. _____

# VII

# Confirming Your Top Five Values

## A. Are they truly your values?

For your values to be pragmatic and real to you, you have to be reflective and thoughtful about how you interpret each of your top values. Also, you need to confirm that these values are, indeed, useful in your day-to-day decision-making and behavioral choices. If a value is not useful, then you need to revalidate whether the value is important and perhaps reprioritize your list. Typically, we behave naturally and consistently with our top five values.

List again your five top-prioritized values:

1. _____

2. _____

3. _____

4. _____

5. _____

For each value, complete the table below.

---

Value _____ is important to me because _____.

I have employed this important value over the past year in the following ways:

      (1) I used it when I decided to _____.

      (2) It affected my behavior by _____.

      (3) (Optional) An instance when I took a stand or took part in some action based on this value: _____.

      (4) (Optional) I became angry or exasperated with people who did not live up to this value because _____

---

Repeat the process shown in the box for each of your top five highest-prioritized values.

Make sure each of your values is an end in itself. Said another way, a value is a means if it is used to accomplish another value. If this condition exists, then select another value to be accomplished as an end.

If your top values are in conflict or not demonstrable when assessed here, please go back to section V and revise your priority values. Then, revise section VI, and this section again.

## B.  Value dilemmas

You might find yourself in a situation where two meaningful values are in conflict, and you must resolve opposing pulls. These instances are real dilemmas. For instance, do you show an employee justice or mercy in a case of an honest mistake or wrongdoing? Do you avoid or confront someone where a value issue is at stake? Another example might be honesty and loyalty in the business world. Assume you are the accountant and you have proof the company is committing fraud. Do you report it (honesty) or do you say nothing (loyalty to the company)? Which value prevails? It seems there is no best path. Often it requires thinking about consequences and making compromises. Ask yourself what kind of person you really want to be in terms of character and reputation; that is, with which choice can you best live with yourself tomorrow.

## C. Reflect on your top five values and how they are related to who you are and where you are going

Reflection calls for careful and thoughtful consideration of each of your top values. Take a few minutes to ask yourself how each of these top five values is related to who you are. For example, how does this value impact your life's purpose or direction?

## D. Signify how your top values inspire or motivate you

Ask yourself what it is about each of your top values that causes or arouses a quickening feeling, causes a feeling of confidence or rightness, or causes you to want to take action in some way? If one or more of your top selected values do not do this, reconsider whether it is truly a heartfelt, worthy value you believe is meaningful.

# VIII

## Exercise: Validating Your Values

Give your honest opinion of the four characters depicted in the following story considering the list of values in section V.

## NARRATIVE

"THE SHERIFF OF NOTTINGHAM CAPTURED LITTLE JOHN AND ROBIN HOOD AND IMPRISONED THEM IN HIS DUNGEON FOR STEALING FROM THE RICH CITIZENS OF NOTTINGHAM.

MAID MARION WAS SINGLE AND HAD NEVER MARRIED. SHE WAS IN LOVE WITH ROBIN AND BEGGED THE SHERIFF FOR THEIR RELEASE. SHE DESPISED THE SHERIFF AND ACTUALLY WAS SECRETLY SUPPORTIVE OF ROBIN AND LITTLE JOHN'S ENDEAVORS.

THE SHERIFF WHO HAD ALWAYS WANTED TO MARRY MAID MARION TO HELP HIS PERSONAL AMBITIONS AGREED TO RELEASE THEM ONLY IF MAID MARION SPENT THE NIGHT WITH HIM. MARION KNEW WHAT THIS MEANT AND RELUCTANTLY AGREED.

THE NEXT MORNING THE SHERIFF KEPT HIS WORD AND RELEASED ROBIN AND LITTLE JOHN. UPON HIS RELEASE AND MEETING MARION, ROBIN WAS INSISTENT THAT MARION TELL HIM HOW SHE PERSUADED THE SHERIFF TO FREE THEM.

MARION TOLD ROBIN THE TRUTH, AND WAS SHOCKED WHEN HE VERBALLY ABUSED HER, CALLING HER AN UGLY NAME, AND SAYING THAT HE NEVER WANTED TO SEE HER AGAIN.

LITTLE JOHN WAS DISAPPOINTED IN ROBIN'S REACTION AND DEFENDED HER, INVITING HER TO LEAVE WITH HIM AND PROMISING LIFE-LONG DEVOTION. SHE ACCEPTED AND THEY RODE AWAY TOGETHER. IT WAS ONLY LATER THAT MARION FOUND OUT THAT LITTLE JOHN HAD LEFT HIS COMMON LAW WIFE AND CHILD FOR HER."

From the narrative, rank Robin, Marion, Little John and the Sheriff in the order in which you liked them:

| | | | |
|---|---|---|---|
| 1. | Most liked | : | _____ |
| 2. | Second most liked | : | _____ |
| 3. | Third most liked | : | _____ |
| 4. | Least liked | : | _____ |

Why did you pick your *first* choice?

What values did he or she represent and what values did he or she not represent?

In the table below indicate your ranking of each character and cite some values they represented and did not represent to you:

| Character | Rank | Values Represented | Values Not Represented |
|---|---|---|---|
| Robin | | | |
| Marion | | | |
| Little John | | | |
| Sheriff | | | |

The Robin Hood story was adapted from http://www.personalityquiz.net/relational/robinhood.htm

For other exercises see "Values Clarification" by Simon, Howe, and Kirschenbaum (1995)

And, with due credit to *The Merry Adventures of Robin Hood of Great Renown in Nottinghamshire* the great 1883 novel by the American illustrator and *writer* Howard Pyle.


Please complete the above exercise before you continue reading.


Return to your chosen top values and determine how your values might have compelled you to select your ranking in the Robin Hood exercise.

Most people find that their own personal values impact how they rank and ascribe values to the characters in this exercise. How did your choice of values represented by the characters in this narrative align with your own personal values? Generally, we tend to like the people like us and dislike the people who are different from us. Think about your favorite movie or television show and your favorite character, and ask yourself what this says about your values.

You may wonder if there is a right answer to this exercise. The truth is, there is no single right answer. The answer lies within each of us. Consider once more Churchill's quote about courage. Studies from prisoners of war and concentration camp survivors indicate that faith allowed them to survive. Many survivors in classified and unclassified studies say that courage comes from faith.

# IX

# Ultimate Objective

## A. Your values in action daily

### 1. To make decisions

Once you have identified or clarified your set of top values, you will likely find yourself considering the strength of your personal values and thinking about how you act on them. Decision-making often involves making trade-offs between our values. Most, if not all, of our decisions are influenced by our values. Values serve as most motivators and predictors of consequences when decisions or choices are made. You will become increasingly aware of the link between your values and choices.

### 2. To set direction or create a vision

We create predictions and foresight of where we desire to be in the future (called envisioning the future) and set a direction to achieve that vision. We create plans to carry out achieving our future vision. This is not particularly new. What is new, however, is understanding the relationship between your values and your envisioned future. A vision becomes a personal choice, which reflects choosing among values. If highly meaningful values come in conflict with a chosen vision, it is unlikely that vision will be realized. In other words, our vision of the future and our values must be congruent.

### 3. To establish priorities

We constantly prioritize our activities by using our clarified values, which help us decide which priorities are most important to accomplish and in what order. Our values also help us de-conflict competing priorities.

Hence, you need to know and verify that your top values are indeed significant drivers in the decisions and choices you are making; otherwise, you may need to reconsider your chosen top values.

## 4. Integrity and Character

Integrity is one of the most important and oft-cited references to character, reputation, and trustworthiness. Integrity is about having internal consistency in words and deeds, being true to yourself, and maintaining a strict adherence to morally upright principles. Being honest, on the other hand, is *externally* portrayed truthfulness, while integrity is *internally* being truthfully upright with yourself. In order to have a high degree of integrity in your life, knowing what values are meaningful becomes important. Your chosen values about what is morally right and wrong are the foundation of your integrity. Accordingly, your values are the pathway to integrity.

## 5. To establish personal, value-driven goals

Effective people use personal goals as guideposts to organize their lives and yield longer-term direction and shorter-term motivation. Your choices about your personal goals are value-driven. Setting goals involves making decisions—that is, being clear about what you want, which is structured from knowing your values and making predictions about how challenging and achievable they are. Setting goals also involves making choices that are based on your values. If your values are in conflict with any personal goal, it is unlikely the goal will be achieved, if even implemented. Goals and objectives that are closely aligned with your values will likely be accomplished.

# X

# Power of Values to Shape and Focus Our Lives

We are all very different people, and so our top values are different. We must ask ourselves from time to time about the purpose of our lives, about our purpose in leading or managing others. To find this purpose, we must first understand ourselves. You cannot adopt someone else's values or purpose because, as we said, we are all very different people. We must first understand our underlying drives and ourselves. We can shape our purpose by clarifying and understanding our values and how they motivate us. Finding our purpose is neither easy nor quick, but knowing what our values are is an essential step in shaping and focusing our purpose and reason for being.

# XI

## Summary

We have attempted to guide you, the reader, through a process of clarifying and validating your top values. If you have diligently worked through the clarification and validation process, you should now have a stronger understanding of your top values and how they impact your work and life. If you lead and manage on a daily basis, these values will help you make better choices and decisions that positively impact others' lives. You will also notice more effective organizational performance.

People, especially leaders, are defined by their values. Values help adjust your moral compass and, for this reason, are clearly connected with your decisions. Clarifying and knowing your values is crucial in deciding among the multitude of choices you make daily. Our values serve as a "hidden hand" when we make daily choices about operational directions and human activities. We rely on our values to organize our time, make resource trade-offs, prioritize, and provide longer-term direction, planning, and envisioning the future. Thus, knowing and acknowledging our top values have a direct impact on our achieving desired performance outcomes and realizing success.

# Acknowledgments

We want to thank the hundreds of people between 2009 and 2012 who beta tested our values prioritization matrix and contributed to improving our material. In particular, we thank the following five individuals for their peer review and their many improvement suggestions:

**Nathan Grossman, MD,** has been at the helm of Florida's Marion County Health Department since the summer of 1984. From 1994 to 1996, he was also assistant district administrator for health under the old Department of Health and Rehabilitative Services. Dr. Grossman earned a bachelor's degree in zoology, *magna cum laude*, from the University of Vermont in 1972, and his MD in 1977 from Meharry Medical College in Nashville, Tennessee. His honors include membership in Phi Beta Kappa and the Alpha Omega Alpha Honor Medical Society. He was the recipient of the Lange Medical Publications Award in medical school; a certificate of appreciation for Victims' Rights Week from the Office of the State Attorney (1990), 5th Judicial Circuit; Ocala/Marion County Economic Development Council Healthcare Industry Award (1995); Marion County Medical Society Outstanding Leadership Award (2001/2002); and the United Way of Marion County Bonnie Heath Award of Excellence (2004). His additional associations include the Florida Public Health Association, American Public Health Association, National Association of County and City Health Officials, Marion County Medical Society, Florida Medical Association, American Medical Association, United Way of Marion County (board member), Public Policy Institute of Marion County (board member), Early Learning Coalition of Marion County (board member), and Success by 6 of Marion County (Leadership Council chair).

**Gerald T. Hannah, PhD,** is president and CEO of the Gerald Hannah Group (GHG) located in Atlanta, Georgia. GHG provides executive coaching, leadership development, and other management consulting services. He has proven abilities in facilitating learning in leadership, management, ethics, behavioral competency models, team performance, and talent management. Dr. Hannah has either authored or co-authored four books and over twenty professional journal articles and book chapters. He has held senior positions in a private corporation, international consulting firm, and state government. His career includes serving as SR/VP executive and leadership development and succession management for UMB Financial Services, senior consultant with the Hay Group, and state commissioner, Kansas State Commissioner of Mental Health and Mental Retardation.

**Katherine P. Mason, EdD, RN,** is a is a professor at Florida State University College of Nursing in Tallahassee, Florida. Dr. Mason graduated from Duke University School of

Nursing with a BSN degree, earned a master's degree in public health, a degree in nursing from the School of Public Health at the University of North Carolina, Chapel Hill, and an EdD in educational leadership from the University of Florida.

She served as the dean of the Florida State University College of Nursing from 2001 to 2007, the director of public health nursing and performance improvement for the Florida Department of Health from 1989 to 2001, and the director of nursing at the University of North Florida from 1983 to1987. Dr. Mason has over twenty-one years of experience in nursing education. She currently teaches undergraduate public health nursing, leadership, and health care systems courses as well as graduate courses in organizational systems, nursing education, and public health nursing. Her research interests include organizational performance improvement, nursing history, public health, and public health nursing. Current scholarly projects include researching the history of public health nursing in Florida. She has been a journal reviewer for *Public Health Nursing* and an editorial board member of the *Journal of Community Health Nursing*.

Dr. Mason served as the president of the Florida Nurses Association from 1989 until1999 and has served on numerous local, state, and national public health and nursing committees and councils. She has received many honors, including selection as a scholar in the Center for Disease Control Public Health Leadership Institute, 1997, and membership in the Great 100 Nurses in Florida in 2009.

**Mark J. Safferstone, PhD,** is the executive director of University of Mary Washington (UMW) Dahlgren Campus, which is the university's third campus. Mark's primary responsibilities include implementing an effective business development and community engagement strategy, assessing regional educational needs and research opportunities, and working directly with the campus construction project team.

Mark was a member of the university's business administration faculty in 1997 and joined the administrative staff of what is now the UMW Stafford Campus the following year. In this capacity, he served as associate dean and directed the university's professional development programs.

Mark completed his bachelor's degree and master of education degree at the University of Miami, his PhD at Vanderbilt University, and his MBA at the University of Mary Washington.

**Akiva Turner, PhD, JD, MPH,** is currently the communicable disease director, Florida's Broward County Health Department, where he provides leadership and oversight for HIV/AIDS, TB, refugee health, hepatitis, STDs, immunizations, pharmacy, and epidemiology programs. He supervises program directors and works with federal, state, and local agencies. He also serves on state and county policy committees and the Institutional Review Board.

Dr. Turner has served in senior leadership positions in California, Florida, and New York, ranging from adjunct faculty to chief executive officer. His previous experiences include serving as deputy general counsel for mental health/chief privacy officer, NYC Department of Health and Mental Hygiene; chief executive officer, AG Holley Hospital, Florida Department of Health where, among other things, he provided policy/privacy/bioethics consults; Liberty County Florida Health Department director; and executive director, New York State Task Force on Life and the Law, where he advised government officials, professional organizations, and community groups on bioethics and health policy issues.

He earned his juris doctor in 1999 at Benjamin N. Cardozo School of Law, Yeshiva University, New York, New York. He received his doctor of philosophy in medical anthropology in 1994 from the University of California Los Angeles. He was awarded his master of public health in 1992 from the University of California Los Angeles. He received his bachelor of arts in anthropology in 1989 from California State University Long Beach, *magna cum laude.*

# About the Authors

**William O. Blackwood** is the owner of DWB & Associates, a service-disabled Vietnam veteran–owned small business that specializes in quality management implementation, organizational assessment and development, business process reengineering, executive coaching, and strategic planning.

Bill has over thirty-five years of experience in various capacities in both the public and private sectors. He has designed and established quality programs, directed and managed organizational and managerial analyses, planned and successfully implemented large organizational change projects, and established successful strategic planning processes.

Bill earned his undergraduate degree at Norwich University and his master's and doctoral degrees at the University of Florida. Besides his full-time job, he served as a university trustee, member of the National Research Council, Malcolm Baldrige National Quality Award examiner, and a United States Senate Productivity and Quality Award examiner for Virginia. He holds numerous certifications for a wide variety of assessment instruments as well as a number of professional society memberships.

**L. Ray Mauser** is an executive coach, leadership developer, researcher, and consultant. He works with leaders and managers to see bigger, more inclusive perspectives and to think in more creative and collaborative ways about change and the challenges they face. He has conducted personalized one-on-one coaching with dozens of senior leaders and executives.

Ray conducts numerous workshops and training in leadership development and managerial effectiveness. He has facilitated strategic planning seminars and has extensive experience in workshop design, development, and presentation. He has delivered workshops and seminars in leadership effectiveness, influence and persuasion, strategy, organizational development, planning, and change management with a focus on ethics, values, and diversity.

Ray earned his MBA and is an experienced certified integral coach. He served as a senior consultant for the Hay Group for over ten years, where he worked with senior leaders and organizational clients in effecting a wide variety of organizational development and change initiatives as well as developing leaders and managers. He has over twenty-five years' experience in leadership and management development. He currently runs a service-disabled, veteran-owned business engaged in managerial development and executive coaching. He is a member of several professional organizations, including the AMA, ASTD, and ICF.

# Disclaimers

The views expressed here represent our views and do not necessarily represent the views of any organization with which we are or have been affiliated.

Any errors or omissions are solely ours. Throughout the book we have tried to avoid the awkward use of dual pronouns such as "he or she," "him or her," and so forth. Our pronoun choices, when used, are random.

# Notes

The authors encourage your comments and feedback, and we appreciate your corrections or suggestions for improvement of future editions.

# Book Orders

To obtain copies of this book, please contact the authors:
William O. Blackwood
PO Box 1254
Haymarket, VA 20169-3252

Bill@DWB-Associates.com

Or

L. Ray Mauser
8501 Grigsby Drive
Springfield, VA 22152

ray.mauser@verizon.net

# Appendix 1

# Values in Professions

## A. Types of Values

1. **Nursing values, from Florida State University College of Nursing, 2003, include the following:**

   - Caring – encompasses the nurse's empathy for and connection with the patient,

   - Altruism – is a concern for the welfare and well-being of others,

   - Autonomy – is the right to self-determination,

   - Human Dignity – is respect for the inherent worth and uniqueness of individuals and populations,

   - Integrity – is acting in accordance with an appropriate code of ethics and accepted standards of practice, and

   - Social Justice – is upholding moral, legal, and humanistic principles.

2. **National Society of Professional Engineers (NSPE) – Professional Obligations**

   a. Engineers shall be guided in all their relations by the highest standards of honesty and integrity.

      1. Engineers shall acknowledge their errors and shall not distort or alter the facts.

      2. Engineers shall advise their clients or employers when they believe a project will not be successful.

      3. Engineers shall not accept outside employment to the detriment of their regular work or interest. Before accepting any outside engineering employment, they will notify their employers.

4. Engineers shall not attempt to attract an engineer from another employer by false or misleading pretenses.

5. Engineers shall not promote their own interest at the expense of the dignity and integrity of the profession.

b. Engineers shall at all times strive to serve the public interest.

1. Engineers are encouraged to participate in civic affairs; career guidance for youths; and work for the advancement of the safety, health, and well-being of their community.

2. Engineers shall not complete, sign, or seal plans and/or specifications that are not in conformity with applicable engineering standards. If the client or employer insists on such unprofessional conduct, they shall notify the proper authorities and withdraw from further service on the project.

3. Engineers are encouraged to extend public knowledge and appreciation of engineering and its achievements.

c. Engineers are encouraged to adhere to the principles of sustainable development in order to protect the environment for future generations.

1. Engineers shall avoid all conduct or practice that deceives the public.

2. Engineers shall avoid the use of statements containing a material misrepresentation of fact or omitting a material fact.

3. Consistent with the foregoing, engineers may advertise for recruitment of personnel.

4. Consistent with the foregoing, engineers may prepare articles for the lay or technical press, but such articles shall not imply credit to the author for work performed by others.

d. Engineers shall not disclose, without consent, confidential information concerning the business affairs or technical processes of any present or former client or employer, or public body on which they serve.

1. Engineers shall not, without the consent of all interested parties, promote or arrange for new employment or practice in connection with a specific project for which the engineer has gained particular and specialized knowledge.

2. Engineers shall not, without the consent of all interested parties, participate in or represent an adversary interest in connection with a specific project or proceeding in which the engineer has gained particular specialized knowledge on behalf of a former client or employer.

e.  Engineers shall not be influenced in their professional duties by conflicting interests.

   1.  Engineers shall not accept financial or other considerations, including free engineering designs, from material or equipment suppliers for specifying their product.

   2.  Engineers shall not accept commissions or allowances, directly or indirectly, from contractors or other parties dealing with clients or employers of the engineer in connection with work for which the engineer is responsible.

f.  Engineers shall not attempt to obtain employment or advancement or professional engagements by untruthfully criticizing other engineers, or by other improper or questionable methods.

   1.  Engineers shall not request, propose, or accept a commission on a contingent basis under circumstances in which their judgment may be compromised.

   2.  Engineers in salaried positions shall accept part-time engineering work only to the extent consistent with policies of the employer and in accordance with ethical considerations.

   3.  Engineers shall not, without consent, use equipment, supplies, laboratory, or office facilities of an employer to carry on outside private practice.

g.  Engineers shall not attempt to injure, maliciously or falsely, directly or indirectly, the professional reputation, prospects, practice, or employment of other engineers. Engineers who believe others are guilty of unethical or illegal practice shall present such information to the proper authority for action.

   1.  Engineers in private practice shall not review the work of another engineer for the same client, except with the knowledge of such engineer, or unless the connection of such engineer with the work has been terminated.

   2.  Engineers in governmental, industrial, or educational employ are entitled to review and evaluate the work of other engineers when so required by their employment duties.

   3.  Engineers in sales or industrial employ are entitled to make engineering comparisons of represented products with products of other suppliers.

h.  Engineers shall accept personal responsibility for their professional activities, provided; however, that engineers may seek indemnification for services arising out of their practice for other than gross negligence, where the engineer's interests cannot otherwise be protected.

1. Engineers shall conform with state registration laws in the practice of engineering.

2. Engineers shall not use association with a non-engineer, a corporation, or partnership as a "cloak" for unethical acts.

i. Engineers shall give credit for engineering work to those to whom credit is due, and will recognize the proprietary interests of others.

1. Engineers shall, whenever possible, name the person or persons who may be individually responsible for designs, inventions, writings, or other accomplishments.

2. Engineers using designs supplied by a client recognize that the designs remain the property of the client and may not be duplicated by the engineer for others without express permission.

3. Engineers, before undertaking work for others in connection with which the engineer may make improvements, plans, designs, inventions, or other records that may justify copyrights or patents, should enter into a positive agreement regarding ownership.

4. Engineers' designs, data, records, and notes referring exclusively to an employer's work are the employer's property. The employer should indemnify the engineer for use of the information for any purpose other than the original purpose.

5. Engineers shall continue their professional development throughout their careers and should keep current in their specialty fields by engaging in professional practice, participating in continuing education courses, reading in the technical literature, and attending professional meetings and seminars.

3. **The International Coach Federation (ICF) – Core Values**

*Preamble:* We are committed to reliability, openness, acceptance, and congruence and consider all parts of the ICF Community mutually accountable to uphold the following values:

- Integrity: We uphold the highest standards both for the coaching profession and our organization.

- Excellence: We set and demonstrate standards of excellence for professional coaching quality, qualification and competence.

- Collaboration: We value the social connection and community building that occurs through collaborative partnership and co-created achievement.

- Respect: We are inclusive and value the diversity and richness of our global stakeholders. We put people first, without compromising standards, policies, and quality.

4.  **Center for Youth Ethics – Six Pillars of Character**

    In his book, Michael Josephson (2002) cites six pillars (i.e., types of values) associated with character. His professional organization, a center committed to developing character and ethical values in younger, school-aged children, has developed a program called *Character Counts*. The Center for Youth Ethics' six pillars are as follows:

    - **Trustworthiness** (includes honesty, integrity, loyalty, and reliability)

    - **Respect** (includes civility, courtesy, decency); dignity and autonomy; and tolerance and acceptance)

    - **Responsibility** (includes accountability, pursuit of excellence, and self-restraint)

    - **Fairness** (includes open process, impartiality, and equity)

    - **Caring** (includes benevolence or altruism and love)

    - **Citizenship** (includes civic duty and how to behave as part of a community)

# Appendix 2

# Terms Often Defined as Values

## A. Terms frequently defined as values

### 1. Behaviors viewed as values

Behaviors are a person's observable or recordable actions or reactions in response to external or internal stimuli. While other people can observe your behavior, a value is internal and therefore hidden. As you review these behaviors, keep the following question in mind: Is this an observable action that others can see?

| Behavior | Explanation |
|---|---|
| Acceptance | Having a favorable reception to something |
| Assertiveness | Behaving with self-confidence, assurance, and poise |
| Camaraderie | Behaving with goodwill and lighthearted rapport among friends |
| Charitable | Responding with altruism or charity |
| Citizenship | Exercising one's duties, rights, and privileges as a citizen |
| Comforting | Being kind and compassionate |
| Community | Sharing through participation and fellowship with others |
| Consistency | Showing uniformity in successive results or events |
| Courtesy | Demonstrating civility or consideration for others |
| Decency | Conforming to prevailing standards of propriety or modesty |
| Dependability | Showing them reliable, steady, and responsible |
| Dignity | Being gracious, proper, and self-respecting |
| Discerning | Being sensitive or astute; perceptive |
| Encouragement | Inciting another to action or to practice |
| Ethical | Behavior based on one's choice of what is right and wrong, judged by others |
| Generosity | Being charitable, kind, and giving |
| Gratitude | Showing thankfulness and appreciation |
| Hardworking | Observable response of person to an event; industrious, tireless |
| Helpful | Showing acts of caring support; being obliging, accommodating, and cooperative |
| Kindness | Being beneficent and helpful; no requirement exists |
| Law-abiding | Abiding by the encoded rules of society; enduring, lasting |
| Moral | Behavior based on externally established beliefs about what is right and wrong |
| Nurturing | Cultivating, supporting, and encouraging someone's development |
| Preparedness | Being organized and ready |
| Repentance | Acting with remorse or contrition for past conduct |
| Risk adverse | Seeking security |
| Supportive | Taking action to furnish support or assistance to others |
| Sharing | Participating with others, in turns, or using and experiencing jointly |
| Traditional | Observable customs, rituals, habits, and accustomed practices |

## 2. Attitudes viewed as values

Attitudes are a "stable cluster of feelings and behavioral intentions towards specific people, things, or events." See the New Jersey Institute of Technology (NJIT) web site in references.

For instance, an attitude is a disposition or tendency representing an individual's *degree* of like, dislike, or ambivalence for an item, often representing a judgment. As you review these attitudes, keep the following question in mind: Does the attitude form a stable judgment using degrees of likes, dislikes, or ambivalence?

| Attitude | Explanation |
|---|---|
| Cheerful | Being upbeat and joyful (changeable) |
| Continuous Learning | Gaining knowledge, constantly improving, and moving forward toward personal growth |
| Cooperative | Associating and interacting willingly with others |
| Curious | Exploring, questioning; being nonjudgmental, open-minded |
| Democratic | Valuing social equality and respect for citizens |
| Easygoing | Being relaxed or informal in attitude or standards |
| Fun | Engaging in an event seen as enjoyable, exciting, or amusing |
| Goodwill | Wishing for good things to happen to people |
| Hopeful | Judging that something desired can be had or will happen; expectation, faith |
| Joyful | Experiencing elation or intense or exultant happiness |
| Loving | Experiencing an intense desire and attraction toward a person or idea (changeable) |
| Playful | Engaging with other people in a good-humored, lively way |
| Pleasant | Being amiable, friendly, congenial, and affable |
| Respectful | Judging another with a high opinion, regard, honor, admiration, or esteem |
| Reverent | Expressing admiration, awe, or veneration for someone or something |

## Attributes viewed as values

An attribute—an inherent quality or personal characteristic—is often used to describe someone *else*, whether the person being described agrees with it or not. For example, he is an unusually quick thinker, or she is very honest. As you review these attributes, ask yourself the following questions: Can these qualities (i.e., attributes) be used to describe someone else? Can they be considered as belonging to someone else?

| Attribute | Explanation |
|---|---|
| Appreciative | Grateful or thankful to others |
| Attentive | Observant, attending, considerate, and responsive |
| Authentic | Genuine; no phoniness |
| Balanced | Poised, steady, and focused |
| Benevolent | Performs kind, charitable acts |
| Chaste | Virtuous, of good character, and obedient |
| Civil | Polite, courteous, and gracious; having good manners |
| Clear Thinker | Acts intelligently without mental confusion |
| Committed | Bound emotionally or intellectually to a course of action; vow |
| Competent | Adequate or well-qualified; capable, able, and proficient |
| Conceptual thinker | Has ideas that are derived or inferred from specific instances or occurrences |
| Conscientious | Painstaking, careful, and diligent |
| Consistent | Steadfast in purpose, constant, and showing evenness |
| Credible | Believable and trustworthy |
| Decisive | Displays certainty, purpose, and resolve |
| Deliberate | Thoughtful, slow, calculating, and unhurried in actions |
| Dependable | Reliable |
| Devoted | Committed to friends or a particular activity; devout |
| Faithful | Adheres firmly to an idea, person, or something eliciting one's fidelity |
| Generous | Liberally gives, shares, or shows big-heartedness |
| Genuine | Unpretentious; similar to authentic |
| Giving | Voluntarily transfers knowledge or property without expecting something in return |
| Good | Morally upright and worthy because of kind, thoughtful acts |
| Honorable | Fair, principled, decent, and worthy of emulation |

| Intuitive | Instinctive, discerning, and insightful |
|---|---|
| Moderate | Has or shows neither too little nor too much of anything |
| Obedient | Compliant, dutiful, subservient, and often unquestioning |
| Patient | Accepts delay, suffering, or annoyance without complaint or anger |
| Principled | Has high moral standards; just, fair, and impartial |
| Prudent | Displays foresight and judiciousness; cautious and careful |
| Pure | Morally good, decent, wholesome, and proper |
| Logical | Thinks logically or analytically using good judgment |
| Resilient | Rebounds quickly from misfortune or change |
| Sincere | Frank, candid, earnest; not feigned or affected |
| Strong | Physically or mentally forceful, resilient, or formidable |
| Thoughtful | Attentiveness when not expected; careful thought and regard or concern |
| Virtuous | Highly principled; morally upright |

## 3. Traits viewed as values

Boyatzis (1982, 28) cites McClelland (1951) as defining a trait as "a dispositional or characteristic way in which the person responds to an equivalent set of stimuli." For example, a trait might be a person's good hand–eye coordination (i.e., his or her consistent response to similar stimuli). As you review the following traits, consider the following question: Is this a distinguishing characteristic or quality about a person, often seen as a peculiarity, such as unusual stamina?

| Trait | Explanation |
|---|---|
| Composed | Consistently maintains a tranquil or calm state of mind |
| Creative | Constantly innovative, ingenious, and resourceful; shows originality |
| Diligent | Purposeful, focused, meticulous, and thorough |
| Gentle | Mild, docile, moderate, calm, or kind |
| Ingenuity | Constantly inventive; displays imagination, originality (similar to one who is creative) |
| Objective | Seeing multiple perspectives without emotion |
| Self-control | Consistently controlling impulses and avoiding specific behaviors |
| Stamina | Displays endurance or physical or mental staying power |
| Tranquil | Consistently peaceful or calm; equanimity |

## 4. Other terms viewed as values

Frequently cited as values, these terms are simply typical ways, tests, or means for acquiring something or accomplishing a task.

| Other | Explanation |
|---|---|
| Challenging | Arousing or testing competitive interest or action in difficult but stimulating effort |
| Communication | Meaning is defined and shared between two or more parties |
| Consideration | The act of considering; careful thought; meditation; deliberation |
| Detail | Particulars considered individually and in relation to a whole; minutiae |
| Education | An act having developmental effect on someone's capabilities |
| Efficiency | Producing results with reasonable degree of effort to energy expended |
| Motivation | Driving force causing people to act; the intensity and persistence behind behavior |
| Reconciliation | Adjusting thinking on divergent ideas or position so as to accept or make compatible |
| Results-Focused | Concentrating on achieving a purpose or outcome; not distracted; practical |

# References

Blackburn, Simon, ed. 2005. *Oxford Dictionary of Philosophy* (Second Edition). Oxford: Oxford University Press.

Boyatzis, Richard E. 1982, 28. The Competent Manager: A Model for Effective Performance. New York: John Wiley & Sons

Churchill, Winston. 1937. "Alfonso XIII." *Great Contemporaries.* London: Thornton Butterworth, Ltd.

Frankl, Viktor E. 2006. *Man's Search for Meaning.* Boston: Beacon Press.

Josephson, Michael. 2002. *Making Ethical Decisions: The Basic Primer on Using the Six Pillars of Character to Make Better Decisions, and a Better Life.* Marina del Rey, CA: Josephson Institute of Ethics.

http://web.njit.edu/~rotter/courses/hrm301/lecturenotes/hrm301-6.ppt#256,1, Attitude Defined

Kluckhohn, Clyde. 1951. "Values and Value-Orientations in the Theory of Action: An Exploration in Definition and Classification." In Talcott Parsons & Edward A. Shils (Eds.), *Toward a general theory of action* (pp.388-433). Cambridge, MA: Harvard University Press.

Lencioni, Patrick. 2002a. *The Five Dysfunctions of a Team: A Leadership Fable.* San Francisco: Jossey-Bass.

——. 2002b. "Make Your Values Mean Something." *Harvard Business Review.* Boston: Harvard Business School.

Maslow, Abraham. (1954) 1987. *Motivation and Personality.* New York: Harper and Row.

Rokeach, Milton. 1973. *The Nature of Human Values.* New York: The Free Press.

Raths, Louis E., Merrill Harmon, and Sidney Simon. 1973. *Values and Teaching.* Columbus, OH: Charles E. Merrill Books.

Schwartz, Shalom H. 1992. "Universals in the Content and Structure of Values: Theoretical Advances and Empirical Tests in 20 Countries." In *Advances in Experimental Social Psychology*, edited by Mark P. Zanna, vol. 25. New York: Academic Press.

Simon, Sidney. B., Leland W. Howe, and Howard Kirschenbaum. 1995. *Values Clarification: A Practical, Action-Directed Workbook*. New York: Warner Books.

*Webster's Encyclopedic Unabridged Dictionary. 1996. New Revised Edition. New Jersey: Grammercy Books, Division of Random House. Webster's New World Dictionary. 1980. Second College Edition. New York: Simon and Shuster*

# Bibliography

Blackburn, Simon, ed. 2005. *Oxford Dictionary of Philosophy* (Second Edition). Oxford: Oxford University Press.

Boyatzis, Richard E. 1982. The Competent Manager: A Model for Effective Performance. New York: John Wiley & Sons

Churchill, Winston. 1937. "Alfonso XIII." *Great Contemporaries*. London: Thornton Butterworth, Ltd.

Covey, Stephen R., A. Roger Merrill, and Rebecca R. Merrill. 1995. *First Things First*. New York: Simon & Schuster.

Drucker, Peter F. 1999. "Managing Oneself." *Harvard Business Review* 77 (2): 64–74: and *The Effective Executive,* (2002) New York: HarperCollins.

Flaxington, Beverly D. 2009. *Understanding Other People: The Five Secrets to Human Behavior*. Portland, OR: ATA Press.

Frankl, Viktor E. 2006. *Man's Search for Meaning*. Boston: Beacon Press.

Fritzsche, David. 2004, 60. *Business Ethics: A Global and Managerial Perspective* New York: McGraw-Hill.

http://web.njit.edu/~rotter/courses/hrm301/lecturenotes/hrm301-6.ppt#256,1, Attitude Defined

Josephson, Michael. 2002. *Making Ethical Decisions: The Basic Primer on Using the Six Pillars of Character to Make Better Decisions, and a Better Life*. Marina del Rey, CA: Josephson Institute of Ethics.

Kelman, Herbert. C. 1958. "Compliance, Identification and Internalization: Three Processes of Attitude Change." *The Journal of Conflict Resolution* 2: 51–60.

Kluckhohn, Clyde. 1951. "Values and Value-Orientations in the Theory of Action: An Exploration in Definition and Classification." In Talcott Parsons & Edward A. Shils (Eds.), *Toward a general theory of action* (pp.388-433). Cambridge, MA: Harvard University Press.

Kohlberg, Lawrence. 1976. "Moral Stages and Moralization: The Cognitive-Developmental Approach." In *Moral Development and Behavior*, edited by Tom Lickona. New York: Holt, Rinehart & Winston.

Kouzes, James M., and Barry Z. Posner. 1993. *Credibility: How Leaders Gain and Lose It, Why People Demand It*. San Francisco: Jossey-Bass.

Lencioni, Patrick. 2002a. *The Five Dysfunctions of a Team: A Leadership Fable*. San Francisco: Jossey-Bass.

———. 2002b. "Make Your Values Mean Something." *Harvard Business Review*. Boston: Harvard Business School.

Maslow, Abraham. (1954) 1987. *Motivation and Personality*. New York: Harper and Row.

McClelland, David C. 1951. *Personality*. New York: Holt, Rinehart & Winston.

O'Toole, James. 1996. *Leading Change: The Argument for Values-Based Leadership*. San Francisco: Jossey-Bass.

Rest, James R., Darcia Narvaez, Muriel J. Bebeau, and Stephen J. Thoma, 1999. *Postconventional Moral Thinking: A Neo-Kohlbergian Approach*. Mahwah, NJ: Lawrence Erlbaum Associates.

Rokeach, Milton. 1973. *The Nature of Human Values*. New York: The Free Press.

Raths, Louis E., Merrill Harmon, and Sidney Simon. 1973. *Values and Teaching*. Columbus, OH: Charles E. Merrill Books.

Schwartz, Shalom H. 1992. "Universals in the Content and Structure of Values: Theoretical Advances and Empirical Tests in 20 Countries." In *Advances in Experimental Social Psychology*, edited by Mark P. Zanna, vol. 25. New York: Academic Press.

Simon, Sidney. B., Leland W. Howe, and Howard Kirschenbaum. 1995. *Values Clarification: A Practical, Action-Directed Workbook*. New York: Warner Books.

Van Maanen, John, and Edgar H. Schein. 1979. "Toward a Theory of Organizational Socialization." In *Research in Organizational Behavior*, edited by Barry M. Staw, 1:209–64. Greenwich, CT: JAI Press.

Whetten, David A., and Kim S. Cameron. 2002. *Developing Management Skills* (5th ed.). Upper Saddle River, NJ: Prentice Hall.

*Webster's Encyclopedic Unabridged Dictionary. 1996. New Revised Edition. New Jersey: Grammercy Books, Div of Random House*

*Webster's New World Dictionary. 1980. Second College Edition. New York: Simon and Shuster*

# Selective Index

Made in the USA
Las Vegas, NV
15 March 2021